# BINARY OPTIONS

## THE BEGINNERS GUIDE TO TRADE AND PROFIT

### EDWARD DORSEY

# CONTENTS

*INTRODUCTION*            v

PART I
**TRADING TOOLS AND TRADING STRATEGIES**        1

PART II
**FOREX**        39

PART III
**COMMODITIES**        47

PART IV
**INDICES**        55

PART V
**CONCLUSION**        65

# INTRODUCTION

As a child, I was always fascinated with numbers and the economy. I guess if you love something that much you can be 99% sure you'll be excellent at it. I want to show you my 15-minute (M15) binary options strategy that will start making you profit in binary options trading. It is based on years of experience in market analysis and correlation. With this strategy I have made my future secure.

My house, car, and various holiday trips are all made from binary options trading. Let me be clear. You can't make "easy money" in a couple of days. This takes years of work. You will have to be patient. My primary focus is on binary options as it is one the best ways to making money on the market today. In this book, I will show you how to gain the upper hand and earn some serious money. I can't guarantee 100% success, but, as you will see, success rate is around 90% or above.

In this book I will use various terminologies that are common in trading. Consider it a part of your homework to research the meaning of this terminology to develop your understanding of binary options trading. This is a necessary effort for you to go through if you are to find success in this field. There are various online resources designed to teach you about this investment and trading terminology. After you are up to speed, return to the book with a new understanding of what I am showing you.

Right off the bat, I'd like to show you some screenshots of my profit reports.

| Date | Asset | Value | Operation type | Expiration time | Expiry Value | Amount | Profit | Net profit |
|---|---|---|---|---|---|---|---|---|
| 11.04.2017, 12:26:37 | EUR/USD | 1.06162 | put | 11.04.2017, 12:28:00 | 1.06152 | $ 200.00 | $ 376.00 | $ 176.00 |
| 11.04.2017, 12:26:37 | EUR/USD | 1.06162 | put | 11.04.2017, 12:28:00 | 1.06152 | $ 200.00 | $ 376.00 | $ 176.00 |
| 11.04.2017, 12:26:37 | EUR/USD | 1.06162 | put | 11.04.2017, 12:28:00 | 1.06152 | $ 200.00 | $ 376.00 | $ 176.00 |
| 11.04.2017, 12:26:36 | EUR/USD | 1.06162 | put | 11.04.2017, 12:28:00 | 1.06152 | $ 200.00 | $ 376.00 | $ 176.00 |
| 11.04.2017, 12:26:36 | EUR/USD | 1.06162 | put | 11.04.2017, 12:28:00 | 1.06152 | $ 200.00 | $ 376.00 | $ 176.00 |
| 11.04.2017, 12:26:36 | EUR/USD | 1.06162 | put | 11.04.2017, 12:28:00 | 1.06152 | $ 200.00 | $ 376.00 | $ 176.00 |
| 11.04.2017, 12:26:36 | EUR/USD | 1.06162 | put | 11.04.2017, 12:28:00 | 1.06152 | $ 200.00 | $ 376.00 | $ 176.00 |
| 11.04.2017, 12:26:36 | EUR/USD | 1.06162 | put | 11.04.2017, 12:28:00 | 1.06152 | $ 200.00 | $ 376.00 | $ 176.00 |
| 11.04.2017, 12:26:36 | EUR/USD | 1.06162 | put | 11.04.2017, 12:28:00 | 1.06152 | $ 200.00 | $ 376.00 | $ 176.00 |
| 11.04.2017, 12:26:35 | EUR/USD | 1.06162 | put | 11.04.2017, 12:28:00 | 1.06152 | $ 200.00 | $ 376.00 | $ 176.00 |
| 11.04.2017, 12:26:35 | EUR/USD | 1.06162 | put | 11.04.2017, 12:28:00 | 1.06152 | $ 200.00 | $ 376.00 | $ 176.00 |
| 11.04.2017, 12:26:34 | EUR/USD | 1.06162 | put | 11.04.2017, 12:28:00 | 1.06152 | $ 200.00 | $ 376.00 | $ 176.00 |
| 11.04.2017, 12:26:32 | EUR/USD | 1.06162 | put | 11.04.2017, 12:28:00 | 1.06152 | $ 200.00 | $ 376.00 | $ 176.00 |

| Date | Asset | Value | Operation type | Expiration time | Expiry Value | Amount | Profit | Net profit |
|---|---|---|---|---|---|---|---|---|
| 24.03.2017, 15:18:40 | USD/JPY | 111.189 | call | 24.03.2017, 15:20:00 | 111.1925 | $ 200.00 | $ 370.00 | $ 170.00 |
| 24.03.2017, 15:18:40 | USD/JPY | 111.189 | call | 24.03.2017, 15:20:00 | 111.1925 | $ 200.00 | $ 370.00 | $ 170.00 |
| 24.03.2017, 15:18:40 | USD/JPY | 111.189 | call | 24.03.2017, 15:20:00 | 111.1925 | $ 200.00 | $ 370.00 | $ 170.00 |
| 24.03.2017, 15:18:39 | USD/JPY | 111.191 | call | 24.03.2017, 15:20:00 | 111.1925 | $ 200.00 | $ 370.00 | $ 170.00 |
| 24.03.2017, 15:18:39 | USD/JPY | 111.191 | call | 24.03.2017, 15:20:00 | 111.1925 | $ 200.00 | $ 370.00 | $ 170.00 |
| 24.03.2017, 15:18:38 | USD/JPY | 111.191 | call | 24.03.2017, 15:20:00 | 111.1925 | $ 200.00 | $ 370.00 | $ 170.00 |
| 24.03.2017, 15:18:38 | USD/JPY | 111.191 | call | 24.03.2017, 15:20:00 | 111.1925 | $ 200.00 | $ 370.00 | $ 170.00 |
| 24.03.2017, 15:18:38 | USD/JPY | 111.191 | call | 24.03.2017, 15:20:00 | 111.1925 | $ 200.00 | $ 370.00 | $ 170.00 |
| 24.03.2017, 15:18:37 | USD/JPY | 111.192 | call | 24.03.2017, 15:20:00 | 111.1925 | $ 200.00 | $ 370.00 | $ 170.00 |
| 24.03.2017, 15:18:35 | USD/JPY | 111.1925 | call | 24.03.2017, 15:20:00 | 111.1925 | $ 200.00 | $ 200.00 | $ 0.00 |

If you would like to have this trading history, take the advice in this book seriously and work hard.

| Date | Asset | Value | Operation type | Expiration time | Expiry Value | Amount | Profit | Net profit |
|---|---|---|---|---|---|---|---|---|
| 24.03.2017, 15:18:48 | USD/JPY | 111.1925 | call | 24.03.2017, 15:20:00 | 111.1925 | $ 200.00 | $ 200.00 | $ 0.00 |
| 24.03.2017, 15:18:44 | USD/JPY | 111.1905 | call | 24.03.2017, 15:20:00 | 111.1925 | $ 200.00 | $ 370.00 | $ 170.00 |
| 24.03.2017, 15:18:43 | USD/JPY | 111.1875 | call | 24.03.2017, 15:20:00 | 111.1925 | $ 200.00 | $ 370.00 | $ 170.00 |
| 24.03.2017, 15:18:42 | USD/JPY | 111.187 | call | 24.03.2017, 15:20:00 | 111.1925 | $ 200.00 | $ 370.00 | $ 170.00 |
| 24.03.2017, 15:18:41 | USD/JPY | 111.1875 | call | 24.03.2017, 15:20:00 | 111.1925 | $ 200.00 | $ 370.00 | $ 170.00 |
| 24.03.2017, 15:18:41 | USD/JPY | 111.1875 | call | 24.03.2017, 15:20:00 | 111.1925 | $ 200.00 | $ 370.00 | $ 170.00 |
| 24.03.2017, 15:18:41 | USD/JPY | 111.1875 | call | 24.03.2017, 15:20:00 | 111.1925 | $ 200.00 | $ 370.00 | $ 170.00 |
| 24.03.2017, 15:18:41 | USD/JPY | 111.1875 | call | 24.03.2017, 15:20:00 | 111.1925 | $ 200.00 | $ 370.00 | $ 170.00 |
| 24.03.2017, 15:18:41 | USD/JPY | 111.1875 | call | 24.03.2017, 15:20:00 | 111.1925 | $ 200.00 | $ 370.00 | $ 170.00 |
| 24.03.2017, 15:18:40 | USD/JPY | 111.189 | call | 24.03.2017, 15:20:00 | 111.1925 | $ 200.00 | $ 370.00 | $ 170.00 |

# PART I
# TRADING TOOLS AND TRADING STRATEGIES

## Fibonacci Level

Binary options traders use the Fibonacci retracement levels as support and resistance levels. Because the vast majority of traders follow the same standards for CALL and PUT options, support and resistance levels have become self-fulfilling prophecies. Traders use the Fibonacci levels extended (extensions). Again, the majority watch these levels and appropriate them to set goal winning trades, and therefore this tool becomes a self-fulfilling expectation. In an uptrend, the main idea is to monitor the market to retreat to the Fibonacci support level. How do you find the retracement levels? Click on a sign at the lowest level and drag the cursor to the most recent highest level. After that the retracement levels will be displayed, showing the price and the corresponding level. 0.236 (indicated on the yellow lines) looks like the weakest support/resistance level, while the other levels provide support/resistance at about the same frequency. Although these graphs below show how the market draws typically only at the level of 0.382, it does not mean that the price every time will hit that level and turn around. Sometimes you will get to 0.500 and switch to the second path, which will reach 0.618 and turn, and sometimes it will completely ignore Fibonacci and rush through all the levels. The market will continue an upward trend after finding temporary support.

*A CALL option on EURUSD 1H expiry exit points 1.24545. It was taken at a signal above 0.382 levels. Price went back twice and was rejected at 0.382 degrees*

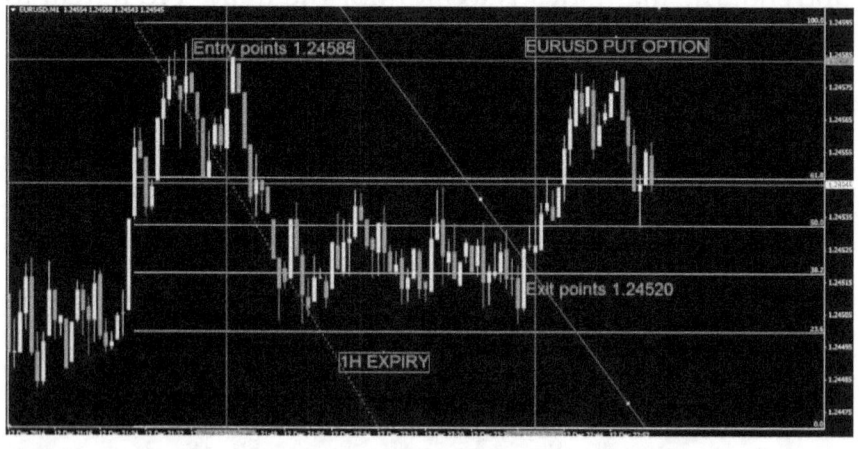

On the image above, you can see the entry points at 1.24585 for PUT option on the EURUSD 1H expiry and exit points at 1.24520. It was taken at a signal above 0.764 extension levels. Price backed twice and rejected from the 0.618 level. It broke the 0.500 level and the price consolidated at 0.382 level expiry. Fibonacci levels are widely used in technical analysis of financial markets. It is a reliable and accurate trading strategy. The recommended level to enter the position of the M1 charts are at only 38.2 to 61.8 as these are the most accurate in predicting the future of price movements. When the price breaks through the level of 38.2, in most cases it will reach the level of 61.8 before the trend changes. You can see the price sharply dropped from 100 Fibonacci level to the 0 level. EUR/USD fell from 1.09475 to 1.09055. It was a strong support level. The price rejected from 1.09055. It was a little trend correction that signaled for a call option on EUR/USD 2 expiry. The price rose to 0.238 Fibonacci level.

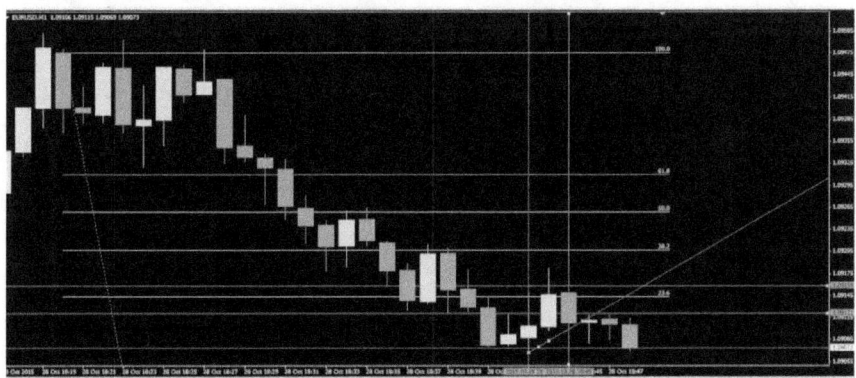

On the M1 charts it showed a negative trend line with very little correction. It was tested again and found a strong support level again.

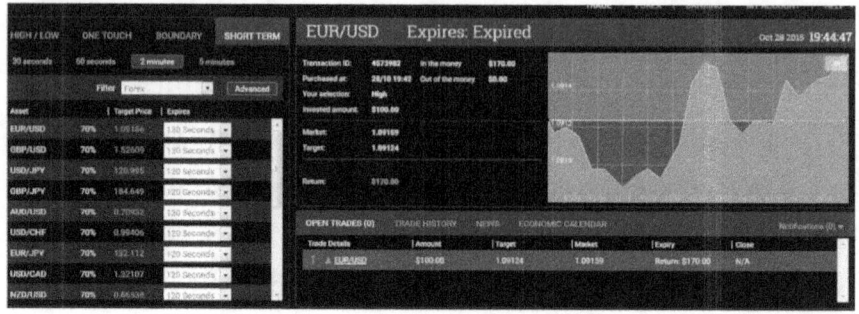

On the image you can see entry points at 1.10124 for CALL option on EUR/USD 2 minutes expiry and exit points at 1.10159. Price backed twice and rejected from the 0.382 level. It was a very short trend correction. It was excellent timing for entry points on EUR/USD. You can see the investment amount of $100 per trade. Trade was recorded in the money 35 points higher than the target price. The payout was 70% and return $170. During the open trade, the price was in the money. This is important because it was too short of time frame for expiry.

The Fibonacci trading strategy can be tested not only for short time frame expiry M5-M15 but also H1, H4, D1, D3, W1. Scalper traders like to use M2-M5 timeframe expiry.

An investor can't lose more money than is paid for call/put

options. If there is a strong movement of the currency pair opposite your position, the risk is limited. Your trade will be recorded out of the money as worthless. If you bought a call option and the price starts to rise, or you purchased a put option, and the price starts to decrease, your potential profit should be unlimited, right? No. This is not the goal with binary options. Trading binary options limits profit and loss. The sum is known from the start. There are different types of binary options. The best known and most commonly used are high/low and touch binary options trading strategies.

If you use high/low, you bet that the price will be higher or lower than the target price at the time of expiry. If you trade a call option and the price at the maturity date is higher than the target price, you will achieve a fixed sum. It does not matter if the price is higher by one point or one hundred points. In both cases you will get the same amount of money. If the price is lower at the time the option expires, you lose the trade. The same principle applies to a put option. The price at the time of expiry should be lower.

Let me show you some advanced insight. The image below is an over uptrend. The candles on the top area are showing consolidation.

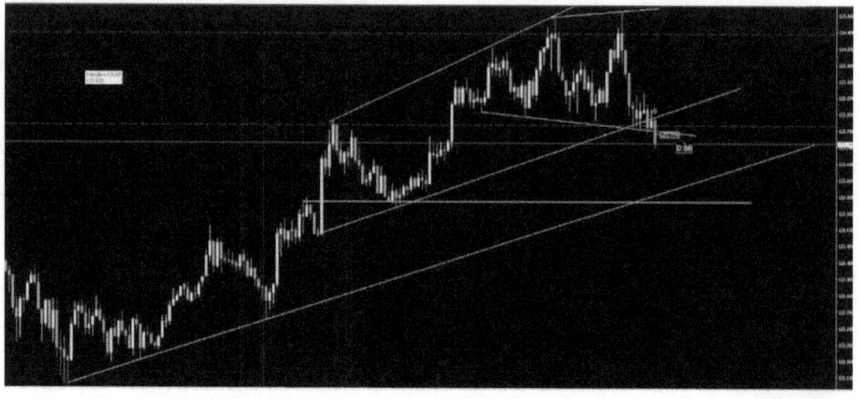

Compare your red line to where I plot mine. The long, slanted treadle below is strong. So, I think that the bear candles can't easily reach it. I was waiting for a breakout, but my target expiry is only very short. It's hard to explain. Part of this comes with experience, but this is how I trade going against the general trend and using micro breakouts for very short expiry targets. This is very advanced, but I hope you will learn something from it. Overall, the trend is bullish, higher lows, higher highs, but the highs aren't increasing as much as before. This is a possible sign of the upward movement slowing down. The last few candles have little movement. The decreased momentum shows signs of rejection from bearish movement as can be seen from the long wicks on the candle before last with long upper wick. This could be a sign of more bearish activity. If the candles come up close under the red line I have drawn then I think it will be bearish for some time. If the candle which still has 2 minutes to go closed above your trend line with a large lower wick, I would say the next two candles will be up.

When you trade with a touch strategy, it is not necessary for a price to be above or below your price at the opening of the expiry of the time. You only need the actual price to reach your predicted price. Let's say the price is currently EUR/USD at 1.08595. You trade an option for 1.08600. Timeout for an hour. Within the hour, the price rises and touches the level of 1.08600. If the price reaches 1.08600 within 15 minutes, you get further gains, and it does not matter what the price will be in 45 minutes. Sometimes high/low options can be riskier than touch options, because the expiration price may exceed the forecast price and come back. In this case, you will lose. If you trade touch binary options, when the price reaches the predicted price, your transaction will automatically be closed and will achieve a profit.

You can also use a technical analysis, which includes tools. The tools are Relative Strength Index (RSI), moving averages, and candlesticks. Also, as previously discussed, Fibonacci retracement is commonly used. It is important to set parameters. For example, Relative Strength index (80,20), moving average (3.16,10), and for Fibonacci the most interesting figures are 38.2 and 61.8 Fibonacci retracements. The best charts are provided by Metatrader (MT4). Using this trading software, you can set up a time frame for one minute, 15 minutes, 30 minutes, one hour, and daily charts, and you can watch the movement of price assets: currencies, commodities, indices, and stocks. It is called a trend. The trend can be ongoing and downward. The ongoing trend is trending when it is forecast that the price will be rising. For a downward forecast the price will fall. When you trade with binary options, you should avoid market overlap and mixed economic data. It causes confusion for traders. Although hedging technique reduces potential losses, it also reduces the potential profit. With these techniques, at the start of trading you may be in profit. Money is in. You watch as you are in the open green position. Then, at the time of close you are in the red position. You are confused and shocked. You were eaten by the market. Why? What did you do wrong? If you played binary options, you can use call and put strategy. Call strategy means that the price will be rising in the future. Put strategy means that it is expected fall in prices in the future.

**How to Make Money Trading Options**

Investing in binary options has become available to anyone.

All you need is a computer, the internet, and some start-up capital. Usually no more than $100 - $ 200. After opening a trading account, you can deposit money. This can be done using several methods, but the easiest way is through credit cards. Trades are executed directly on the site broker.

Strictly speaking, this is investing, not trading. When you invest money, you are not purchasing any goods or currency. Practically, you bet on the movement of prices of certain commodities, indices, or currencies over time. Suppose that it is 6 pm by GMT, and oil prices on the market are at $34. If you believe that the price after a select unit of time (say an hour) should be higher than the site you select, CALL the broker and write down how much money you want to invest. If you think the price will be less than $34.30 after the hour, select and enter the amount to invest. This is it. This is your main job. Now you wait until the time runs out and to see if you were right. If it is, you get 70% - 85% (depending on broker to broker) of what you've invested. For example, if you invested $100, and you were right, you will receive $175. If you did not guess the exact outcome, the broker returns a small portion of the money. From an invested $100, we will be refunded $15.

It is possible to bet on the price movements of currencies

(Forex), the prices of raw materials such as oil, copper, wheat, gold, silver, and many others. There are also well-known stocks and stock indices. It's obvious that this is basically a form of betting. So, never invest more money than you can stand to lose. Learn to predict whether a price or a currency will increase or decrease from its current position. The standard here is 65-70% profit.

In binary options, the most important thing is that you follow the economic data. For this purpose, I use the fxstreet.com bar. There they provide all kinds of charts and data (in real-time mode).

Try to stick to the following schedule on a daily basis. As soon as you earn $40 - $50, or if you lose $40 - $50 just stop. This should not take more than 2 hours a day. Until you master this, and until you gather a little more capital, be very cautious with investments. Invest a maximum of $25 at a time. As soon as you make a little, you STOP. For one day, this is enough in the beginning. At first you are putting into place a basic framework for your mind to understand the patterns. You must learn through experience a little at a time before you can do more. Often those who shoot to earn a lot at once can lose it all in a few minutes. Keep that in mind. If you can be disciplined and follow the above guidelines you will be able to create constant additional capital

**Charting and Patterns**

I have a different approach to drawing support/resistance levels (S/R), because I only use one chart on one time-frame. Also, the way I use S/R is a bit different than how most traders do. I concentrate more on moving S/R and combine it with conventional S/R. The easiest way to learn is to spend lots of hours studying the charts. You'll need to find key levels of S/R on daily charts. Find the current level and one level below the current price.

Doing that on the daily chart might not be enough if you want to trade at 15 min or 30 min, but it is definitely worth studying. Now I'll describe price action trading without using any indicators. I will explain how I take short expiries at 10-15 minutes. In these cases, I still draw lines on the daily chart and sometimes the H4 chart. I am observing S/R levels of the daily chart, the 4-hour chart, and perhaps the 1-hour chart. I wait for the price to get to the S/R areas, and then I look for a long wick pin bar as a signal.

I'm watching the charts. It clearly shows bouncing up and down, where it's struggling to break or it breaks with a fairly large candle. If it does this at least two different times, I draw a line there. The confusion is if they are major or minor breaks. At this point, I am still learning and not actually doing any live trading; I don't have an expiry. My plan is to learn how to plot key S/R levels and do that on multiple charts. It is only a matter of looking at a few times and let the price/chart come to your key S/R levels and then wait for long wick pin bars as a signal. There may be a lot of bounces and then it breaks with a big candle. The key S/R levels on higher timeframes are normally robust, and can be used on lower timeframe trades. If I'm using shorter expiries I can use the S/R from the higher level, which I believe is also the minor S/R. Of course, the higher you go I think you need to concentrate on the major S/R.

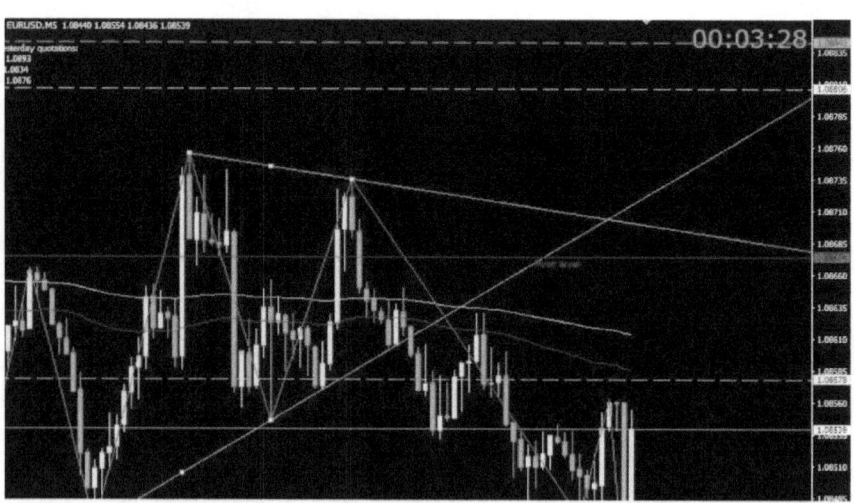

The above image shows something I drew this morning. See the blue lines I drew connecting earlier highs and lows? The yellow dotted line is from the first 4 hours of opening from midnight GMT. I got it from 4 candles, which mark the lowest prices during this time. Now, see the bear candle that closes outside my lower trend line? It would have delivered a good 15 min trade. It could have caught it on the upside when the next bull candle didn't touch the trend line and closed under the exponential moving average (EMA). I missed some good action.

Be sure to spend plenty of time watching candlestick patterns. Go to them before you start using indicators. It's a shame not to use them when there is so much info in there. Watch different variations of a candlestick, and it will tell you most of what you need to know. Backtesting is good, but just be wary of backtesting with moving averages as they don't work the same after the fact. Even if you don't get to trade, watching the charts and seeing what happened is good for learning. Then you can say, "hmmm, every time the price touched that line and closed above, it continued up for x minutes and vice versa."

A candlestick can be formed based on the opening and closing price. It includes the highest and the lowest price of the day. The main patterns worth mentioning are hammer, shooting star, hanging man, and reverse hammer candlesticks. These candles can be used to take a signal. When prices continue to drop hammer sends a signal that is close to the support level. Then price starts to rise again. The shadow shows that sellers pushed prices lower. Buyers wanted to push higher price. Hammer doesn't mean that you should trade call option. It needs to be confirmed before you can trade safely. Hanging Man is indicates the top or a strong resistance level. A long lower shadow indicates the price may push lower. It can be used as a signal for the put option. The inverted hammer shows a declining trend line. It suggests the possibility of reversal. It is a clear signal for a put option.

**Triangle Pattern**

The image above shows a triangle candlestick pattern. It has been broken; so, call option can be used. The symmetrical triangle forms on the chart where the line of the highest prices and lowest price lines converge together to the point where they look like a triangle.

When this formation happens, the market produces lower peaks and higher bottoms. This means that neither buyers nor sellers are pushing prices far enough to achieve a clear trend. If this is a battle between buyers and sellers, then this is considered a draw. This type of activity is called consolidation. On the chart above we can see that buyers and sellers have failed to push the price in their direction.

When this happens, we will get lower peaks and higher bottoms. When the two slopes come closer to one another, it is expected to breakout. We do not know in what direction, but we know it will come to a breakout.

In the end, one side will be surrendered. So, how can we take advantage of this situation? Easy. We can set tasks above the top line and the lower line. Since we know that the price will break through, we can easily set tasks regardless of market direction.

As you probably guessed, the drop-down triangles are exactly the opposite of an ascending triangle. In descending triangles, there are a number of lower peaks that make up the top line. The lower line is the support that the price can't penetrate. If price points gradually this tells us that sellers are now receiving battles as opposed to buyers. In most cases, the price will break the line support and will continue to fall.

However, in some cases the support line is too strong. The price will bounce up and will strongly progress upwards. The good news is that we do not care where the price goes. We know that it will go somewhere. In this case, we set the tasks above the upper line (lower peaks) and below the support line. This formation occurs when there is a level of resistance and a higher bottom line. It will happen that there will be a certain price level that buyers can't move. However, they gradually start to push prices up, as evidenced by a higher bottom.

Take a critical stance, and ask these questions.

- The buyers keep the pressure on the level of resistance, and as a result, a break out will happen. The question is, in which direction?

- Will buyers be able to break the resistance level?

Most books will tell you the price will break through the line of resistance. However, in my experience so far, this is not always the case. Sometimes the resistance level is so strong that there is not enough power with the buyers to push through price line. I want to be ready to move in both directions. In this case, I would make an order above the resistance line and below the support line.

**Stochastic**

The most commonly used stochastic is the slow stochastic. Stochastic oscillators are used to determine the strength of a trend or when approaching the end of a trend. Stochastics are displayed by two lines known as %faster and %slower, that oscillate on a scale of 0 to 100. The mathematics behind the oscillators is unimportant. What is important is the meaning and placement of the lines. When the lines cross above 80, it represents a strong upward trend. When they cross below the 20 line, it represents a strong downward trend. When the %K line crosses the %D line, it could indicate a change in trend and a possible exit point. When prices fluctuate, stochastics will cross over the medium term - which indicates the lack of a trend. The stochastics give their best signal when both the lines are moving to a new level at the same time as the actual price. This is a good indicator of the trend continuing. However, when the stochastics cross in a different direction of a prolonged trend this could be an indication of either exit or switch directions.

In the above image, I didn't get in for a put at 1.08420. At the lower low it's not a good idea. I think it can go up from the lower low. At the time the way I saw it was that the price hadn't been this low since the end of Jan, and although it's higher than that, it is still lower than the most recent low.

From my perspective, I'm not sure if this is right or not, but it could possibly fall further. The risks of the low not being supported is hence higher. This is a game of probabilities. You don't want the odds against you. If the option has strong support, then no problem, but not on a lower low like this. The best thing to do would be waiting for a new support level to be established or to wait for a retracement and then trade put again.

In the image above the price is making higher lows, but also lower highs into the blue triangle my trend lines have created. So the price will break in one direction soon enough, but when the triangle is shaped like this which way does it go? 1hr stochastic is oversold; so, I'm thinking the break will be to the upside. Then again Frankfurt is going to open right now. The price just broke my trend line upwards, but the candle has retreated. When it closes above it might be a sign of upward action.

**Learn how to trade**

With trading platforms you can use a 100% web-based trading platform. There's no need to download anything. On an online platform you can see leaderboards, trading history, market news, special offers, and video tutorials. In the US, there are fewer options for binary options brokers due to the laws in place. However, they do exist. Do your homework to find the best option as there are some options out there that are actually scams.

With the platform in the image above (IQ Option, not available in US), you have options to choose an expiry from 5 minutes to the end of the day/week/month and many options in between, including 10, 15, 30, 45 minute expiries. It can also be used for H1, H2, H4 timeframe expiries. I recommend timeframes from 5 to 30 minutes.

The next step is the investment amount per trade. It is often called risk management. You never risk more than 1.5% to 2% of your account. This amount can go up to 5%, depending on your appetite for risk. At the beginning of your binary options trading, the best to try to maintain it at 1%. Later, as you progress and become a better trader, you can increase the sum of your trade. It is my recommendation that this should still be less than 5%. You probably think that with using 2% of the amount of your account you will never be able to earn money needed to live from binary options trading. This is not true, and. I will show you how to generate earnings using 2% of your account by connecting their gains.

Let's say you have $1,000 per account, 2% of that amount is $20 per trade. So, you enter into the trading positions risking $20. Remember the size of the positions is calculated in accordance with that. After winning several trades, your profit will constantly increase. So, you will risk 2% of the amount new amount, which is greater than $20. It will allow you to trade using a higher position. Of course, your profits will increase. In this way, the trader continues to trade risking 2% of his account. But now those 2% are higher than before when you had $1000 in your account

The downside is that if you have lost a lot, then the 2% of the amount is. Recovery will be more difficult. The trader needs more gains than losses to recover his account to $1000.

You can see in the image the investment amount per trade. Never use more than 5% as risk management. What does this mean? It means the following.

$500 deposited account use $10 per trade=$500x0.02=$10

$700 deposited account use $14 per trade=$700x0.02=$14

$1000 deposited account use $20 per trade=$1000x0.02=$20

$1700 deposited account use $34 per trade=$1700x0.02=$34

$2000 deposited account use $40 per trade=$2000x0.02=$40

$5000 deposited account use $100 per trade=$5000x0.02=$100

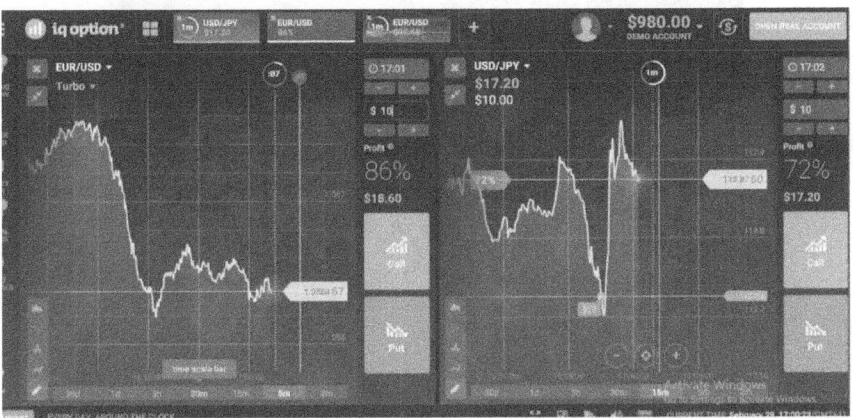

In the image above you can see $1000 deposited in the account. You can use put option on EUR/USD. Press the red button to put, and the trade is executed. This means that the bet is that the price will drop. On the right you can see call option on USD/JPY. To do so you can press the green button, and the trade is executed. Call option means that the bet is that the price will rise. Also, you can see 2% risk management. $10 per each trade. Total investment amount $20 or 2% risk management. You can see the trade status. Both trades are in the money so far.

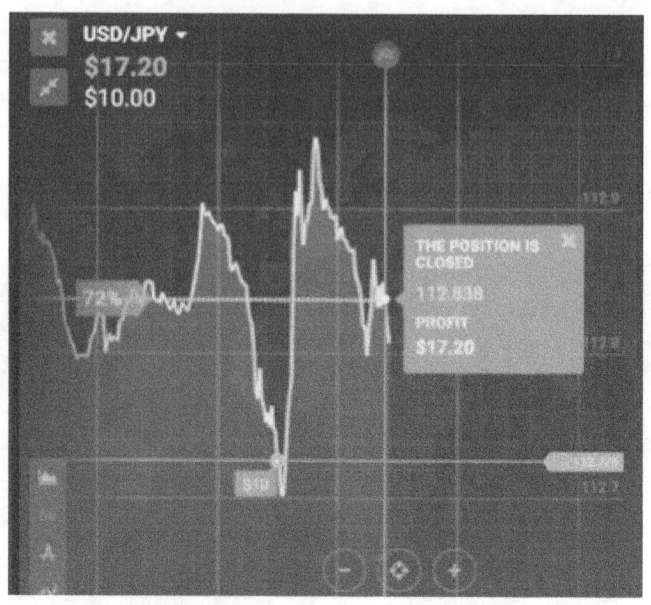

*This image is shows the expiry time. USD/JPY recorded in the money.*

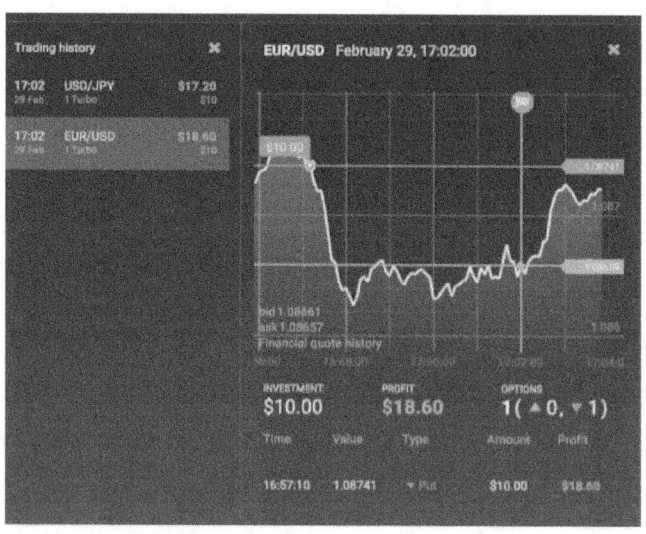

In the above image, the investment amount was $10 per trade. The payout was $86, and return was $8.60. You can see the entry market price at 1.08741 and the expiry price was 1.08659. It can be concluded that the exit points were lower by 82 points.

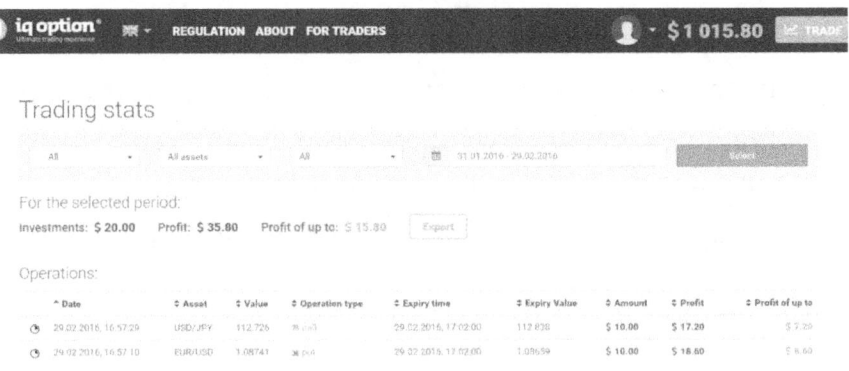

This image shows the trading history and profit. Investment amount was $20 and total profit $15.80. Total profit was $1015.80/$1000=1.0158x100%=1.58% profit on a daily basis.

This trading platform provides the customer with real market price with a demo account. A demo account is the best way to avoid risk on investments and gain valuable experience in binary options trading. It is perfect to learn and to practice trading. A demo account allows you to experience trading in real market conditions without depositing your funds. It has flexible settings which allow you to explore the benefits of trade. A demo account has the same options as a real account. When you have lost lots of virtual money, and when you finally start making money in the demo account, then you can start thinking about opening a real trading account. Be sure not to open a real account if the total trading on demo accounts are not in profit. It simply means that you are not yet ready. Nothing wrong with opening a new demo account and start from scratch. In this case, the only thing you lose is your time. The profit will come with time and practice. The market will be waiting.

This next strategy is based on the currency correlation of EUR/USD and USD/JPY. It can be used for binary options trading on a 5 minute timeframe expiry. Currency correlation means the following, when EUR/USD drops USD/JPY rises. It shows two winning trades and 100% success rate.

**Example 60 Second Trade**

The 60 second trading strategy is for all traders. It's risky, but its payout is 70-85%. First, set up a timeframe expiry of 60 seconds.

| High / Low | One Touch | Range |
|---|---|---|
| 30 SECONDS | 60 SECONDS | 2 MINUTES | 5 MINUTES |

At the start of trading, you need to choose the assets. In this sample it will be EUR/USD. Will the EUR/USD at 60 seconds close higher or lower than the current price? If you think it will be higher you press the high button. If you think it will lower you press the low button.

You select high. Then set up the investment amount. It shows $50 per trade, and the payout is 72% or $86 if it is recorded in the money. Then you press the apply button, and the trade is executed.

If it is in the open green position recorded "in the money" it is a profitable trade. If this switches to the closed red position, "out of the money," the trade is lost. Some traders think that 60 seconds trading strategy is pure gambling. Other traders think it is a very profitable strategy in a short time frame expiry. It's an opportunity to make a lot of money in 60 seconds. A trader who wants a quick turnover of money should be trading with this strategy. One advantage of trading strategies with 60 second expiry binary options is that not a lot of money is required. Trading 60 second binary options can be done with a simple strategy.

**Touch/No Touch Binary Options Trading Strategy**

The touch option has increased in popularity, and is now provided by more and more binary brokers. With the touch option you choose whether or not you believe the property in question will touch a higher or lower level target before the expiration. The outcome depends on whether or not the market price doesn't or can't achieve the target price set at the time of placing before the option expires. These types of options are usually offered on a daily basis or on weekends with a broker setting a target distance. Touch options belong to the most profitable types of binary options on the market at the moment. While standard options trading offers the possibility of payment in the amount of 70 - 80% of the funds invested, at the level of touch option payments can go up to 500% on deposits.

The touch up/down binary options trading strategy is based on the difference in price between market and target price 20 points. The best trading assets for this strategy are EUR/USD, AUD/USD, and GBP/USD. You can see below the good timing for entry points. Market price 1.36198 and target price 1.36178. It is exactly 20 points. 1.36198-1.36178=20 points. This was good timing for entry points touch down on EUR/USD.

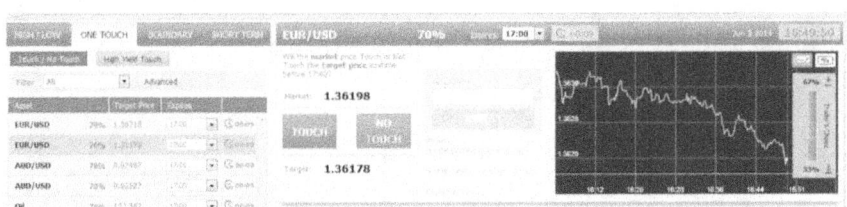

No touch up/down binary options trading strategy is based on the difference in price between the market price and target price 80-100 points. The best trading asset for this strategy is EUR/JPY.

In this image you can see EUR/JPY the market price at 141.762 and target price at 141.701. Difference in prices is 141.762-141.701=61 points. This isn't enough range for entry points for a no touch strategy. It needs to respect the rule of 80-100 points. In the case below it is possible, 139.338-139.245=93 points. This is good timing for entry points.

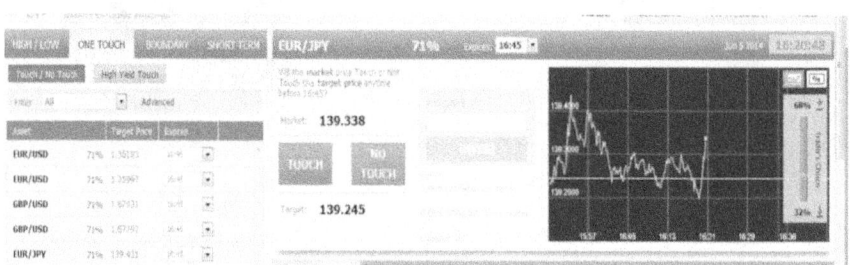

I will show one winning trade and explain what it looks like.

Above you can see no touch down on EUR/JPY at a target

price 141.447 and market price of 141.622. It is recorded in the money. To be recorded in the money, market price can't touch the target price. If it is touched, the trade is lost. In this case, this was a winning the trade.

**Learn when to trade**

Traders usually trade at the wrong time, because they use M1 and M5 charts. A better solution is to use H1 charts for binary options trading. It depends what kind of trader you are. There are traders who prefer M15 charts. So, it is necessary to define the best timeframe charts to use before start trading. The trader should feel comfortable when he is trading. No pressure needed. It is necessary to find the best time for trading. The best time for trading is when London and New York open. The best days for trading are Tuesday, Wednesday, and Thursday. Avoid trading on Monday, Friday, and Sunday. The worst times for trading is during the news and holidays.

The choppy market is when London and New York overlap. It is related to currency pairs. Never trade on Friday. Most traders close at profitable positions in forex trading. When London is closed at 17 GMT, the market becomes quiet and slow. This means that it can be traded only half a day on

Friday. If a trader knows this information, he will make a profit. He can use the best time for trading.

The highest price movement in pairs is on Wednesday and Thursday. GBP/USD has the highest volatility. The second is EUR/USD; the third is USD/CHF. USD/JPY has minimum volatility. A trader can foresee that the highest volatility will be on Wednesday, because of an FOMC statement, interest rate decisions, or the governor of the central banks will speak. If traders decided not to trade on Wednesday when the highest volatility may occur, and easy to make money, it could cause more problems.

On Friday price movements can't be predicted. On this day you can lose your money. Traders wanted to trade on Friday to cut losses. It is usually published by NFP the first Friday of the month. It will be influenced by the market. Currently, the last report was worse than expected. It was disappointing. Traders hoped to the US economy would recover. They wanted to be sure that the global economy is not going toward another financial crisis. It is expected to be 195000 after falling 151000 in the previous month. On Sunday you will start your trade with one or two lost trades. The banks are closed, and there is no trading activity. During the holiday banks are closed. It is the smallest trading volume. It is better not to trade during the holiday. You can go fishing or enjoy life. Trading during the news is bad luck. A trader doesn't know what the price direction will be after published economic data. Price jumps up and down during the news. It is unpredictable.

If you work or sleep in this time zone, you can't trade during the best hours. You can provide yourself with better solutions. You can use London's trading session. You have to change your lifestyle and habits. Trading during work can be bad. What happens if your boss notices what you are doing during the working hours? The employer is paying you to trade instead to work for him. In this case, if you want to trade you have to become a master trader. You can also become position trader and trade when you return from work. If you can't trade during EU and US sessions, you can trade during Asian trading sessions. You have to learn how to read these charts.

When you watch the charts, you can learn the real story of price movements with the assets you trade. It is better to watch live charts than history charts. Practice before you start trading. You will be a better trader this way. You will decide when is easiest to make money based on experience.

If it is a bank holiday in Japan and China, you can safely trade EUR/USD and GBP/USD. Published economic data can only shake the market in the short term. Brokers sometimes work a short time during the Christmas and New Year's holiday. There is no technical and fundamental analysis during this time. So many traders decided to break the trading between Christmas and New Year. The major market players are removed from the market temporarily, but they still hold open profitable positions. From the 15th of December to the 15th of January is the worst time for trading.

It is expected that the UK campaign to stay or leave the EU will affect trade. If the UK leaves the EU there will be the global effects for eurozone countries and the UK separately. Investors have been expecting shock in the market at the global level. When the campaign to leave the EU broke the news, the pound dropped against the US dollar, euro, yen, and the Swiss franc.

Oil is still in a declining trend line. It is being discussed whether to cut oil production. Saudi Arabia and Russia are concerned. They expect that the price will reach $45-$50 per barrel this year. Iran also started to sell oil in the global market. Sanctions have been suspended. The oil prices are still lower with a smaller correction. So far, there is no clear answer what the future will bring.

Gold continues to rise. Gold is a safe trading instrument during crises like a slowdown of the Chinese economy and events in the Middle East. It is expected that gold will rise. The price of gold will be affected by the slowdown of the Chinese economy and hike rate in the US. China and India are the largest gold buyers. This could cause increased demand for this precious metal. In this case, the gold price will rise. If the Fed continues to hike rates in 2016, the US dollar will be stronger. The price of gold will drop. There is an inverse correlation between the US dollar and gold. If the US dollar rises, gold drops. If the gold rises, the US dollar is weaker and drops.

All of the above needs to be taken into account when determining when to trade. It may be overwhelming at first, but over time it becomes manageable.

# PART II
# FOREX

I will explain currency correlation between two pairs USD/CHF and GBP/USD. If USD rises, GBP drops and vice versa. You can see in the image below currency correlation between two pairs. Two trades are recorded in the money.

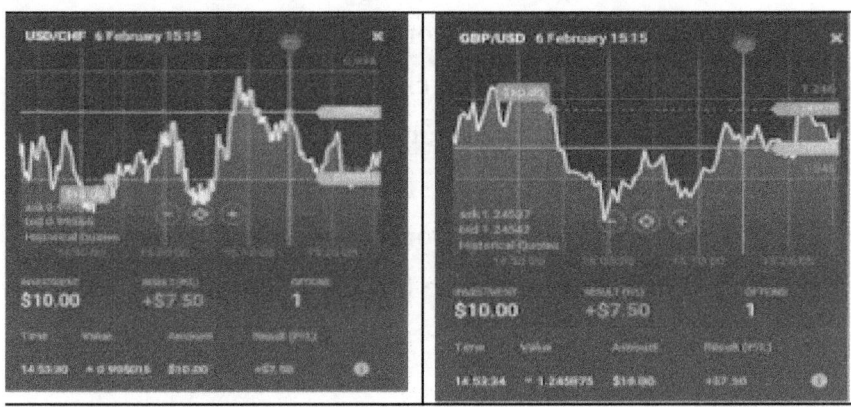

*Currency correlation USD/CHF call option and GBP/USD put option 15 minutes time frame expiry*

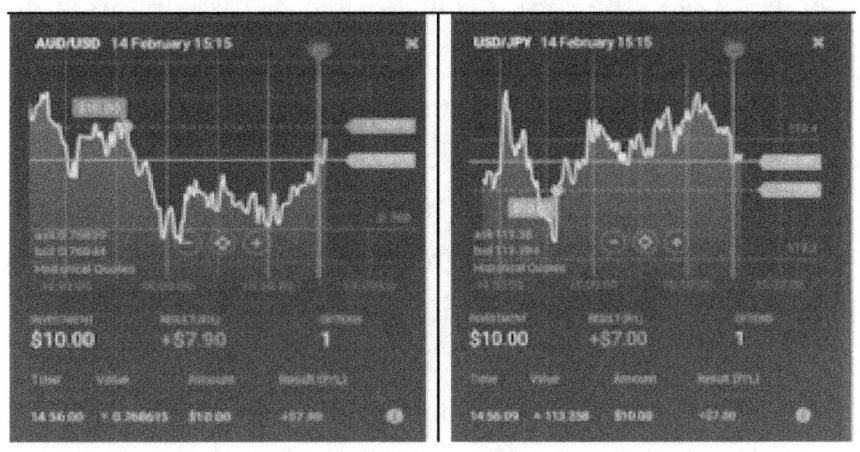

*If USD rises, AUD drops as well as EUR, YEN, GBP, NZD, CAD...*

Relative Strength Index (RSI) is one of the leading trading indicators in the forex market. It is one of the favorite trading indicators for beginner as well as professional options traders. Trading indicators are ready for use to provide trading signals for selling or buying position. RSI is based on the difference between the average closing price during the positive days and the average closing price during the negative days, observed over a period of 14 days. This information is then converted to a value which ranges from 0 to 100 degrees. One of the most important position areas is at 50% of the RSI. It is the neutral area for any position.

When the average wage is higher than the average loss, the RSI rises, and when the average loss is greater than the average wage, the RSI declines. RSI is usually used to confirm an existing trend. The positive trend is confirmed when RSI is above 50, a negative trend when under 50. It can also indicate whether or not a security is being overbought or oversold. At or below 30 it indicates it's being oversold. Above 70 it is being overbought. This warns of an impending reversal. A situation in which there has been too much purchase on the market (RSI above 70) means that the market has almost no customers, and prices are likely to fall since those who have previously purchased now want to make a profit by selling. A situation in which there has been too much selling (RSI below 30) is the opposite. With this information we have our put trading strategy entry points; short if RSI (14) crosses above 70 and then crosses back down again. The full red line crosses the green line for short put strategy. Conversely, the call trading strategy entry points are found when RSI (14) crosses below 30 and then crosses back up again. Full red line crosses over the green line for long trading strategy

*Currency correlation AUD/USD put option and USD/JPY call option 15 minutes time frame expiry*

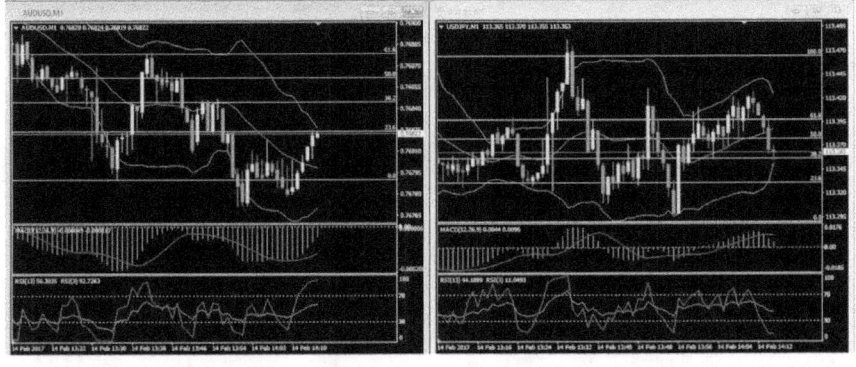

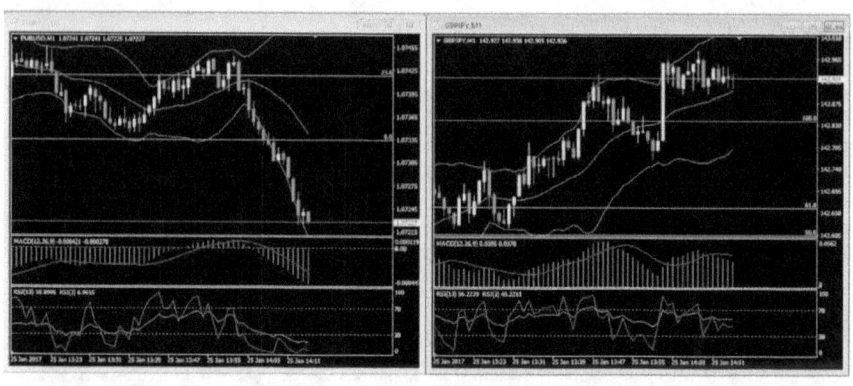

*Entry/exit points and 70% payout.*

In the image above, you can see excellent entry point and put options on EUR/USD. The signal was taken when the price broke the lower Bollinger Bands (B Bands). It also broke 0 Fibonacci level. On the right is a call option on GBP/JPY when the price broke 100 Fibonacci level.

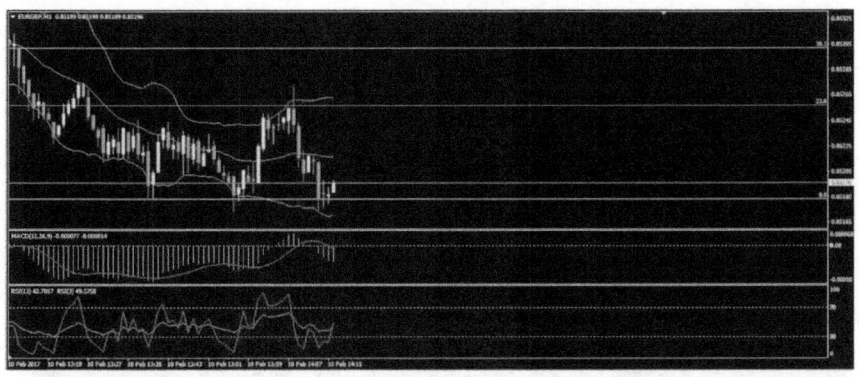

*Call option on EUR/GBP almost 20 minutes time frame expiry.*

# PART III
# COMMODITIES

When the dollar starts to weaken, investors around the world begin to invest more in gold for safety. The increase in demand for anyone going this way affects the growth of prices of the precious metal. When the dollar falls, gold prices will rise. Thus, for our purposes, the price of gold has a small practical value with its primary role of screen values. In situations where the value of money falls about the value of goods and services, people invest in gold to preserve the value of their investment. The amount of inflation is one of the leading factors in the current decision-making on the future monetary policy of large world central banks, including the Federal Reserve. The target value of inflation in the economies of developed countries is about 2%. In the US, the amount of inflation has not reached this level, which is one of the reasons why the Federal Reserve has not yet decided to raise interest rates. Its growth, together with other factors will lead to the normalization of monetary policy, which reflects positively on the dollar and thus lowers the price of gold.

To this day US funds are the most potent drivers of the financial market. The price of gold falls when investors of government bonds become more interested in investing in gold. In periods of high-interest rates, there is a lower level of free capital, which increases the demand for it and, therefore, increases the premium to be paid (interest) to those who are willing to lend their money. The need for gold is falling, and hence, so is its price. Significant events for the price of gold are held by the FOMC (Federal Open Market Committee). They are held eight times a year in the United States. At these events it is determined whether or not to raise the target value inter-bank interest rates and thereby determines whether it will be easier (cheaper) or difficult (expensive) for banks to borrow money from each other. At high-interest rates, if the bank has a shortage of deposits borrowed from the citizens, it is not easy or cheap to borrow money from other banks, which further increases the value of capital and interest rates. This situation does not favor the growth of gold prices.

Between 2010 and 2012 a large number of central banks in developing countries reduced the share of dollars in foreign exchange reserves and increased gold. China has 1.7% of its reserves in gold, India 10%, Brazil 0.5%. In particular, countries with current account deficits such as India (10%), Belarus (30%), Egypt (25%) often prefer gold to stabilize its currency, while the western central banks still hold the previous rules of the IMF and do not buy more gold. Gold reserves in countries that have the status of developing are still relatively low compared to the very high percentages in many European countries. The reason for this is that countries like France, Germany, and Italy have built their reserves during the period of the gold standard. Most central banks in the world still maintain the benchmark interest rate at a record low. The Fed is expected to increase the interest rate which strengthens the dollar and lowers the price of gold.

The increase compared to the imbalance in the USA strengthens the price of gold. The growth in the price of gold usually goes along with the economic growth of developing countries and Europe, and contrary to the economic growth of the United States. The euro has a strong positive correlation with the price of gold; when the euro rises typically so do gold prices. This factor is significant, because it's the indicator for inflation, the intervention of central banks in times of crisis, and the increase in the availability of money, which has a positive impact on the growth of commodity prices. There is a key difference between the growth stimulated by investments in developing countries and growth-induced consumption, which is usually the case in the US, leading to the creation of fear factor due to global imbalances. Growth in investment and real estate prices in the US often weakens the price of gold because they increase the likelihood of interest rate increases.

Factor costs of the exploitation of gold are very high. In the last decade, the demand for gold and copper in China, as well as benchmarks for investments in China, are closely linked. Lower commodity prices and oil prices negatively affect the price of gold. The high level of oil stocks in the US, and the slowdown in the global economy negatively impact the amount of oil and, thus, the price of gold.

Approximately 45% of the annual demand for gold comes from jewelers, 45% from investment, while only 10% is from industrial application. If for any reason one of these areas show growth, demand for gold price rises as a logical consequence of supply and demand. India and China are the most significant buyers of the precious metal in the world. So, economic conditions, as well as their legal regulations, also influence the movement of prices.

The image below shows gold and silver trading. It was used for a call option on gold and silver. Investment amount of gold was $20 while payout was 75% and retained profit was $15. For silver, the investment amount was $30. The payout was 73%, and profit was $21.9. On the M1 charts below, you can see both signals wer taken when the price bounced from the 61.8 Fibonacci level and lower B Bands. All trading indicators confirmed a signal for the call option.

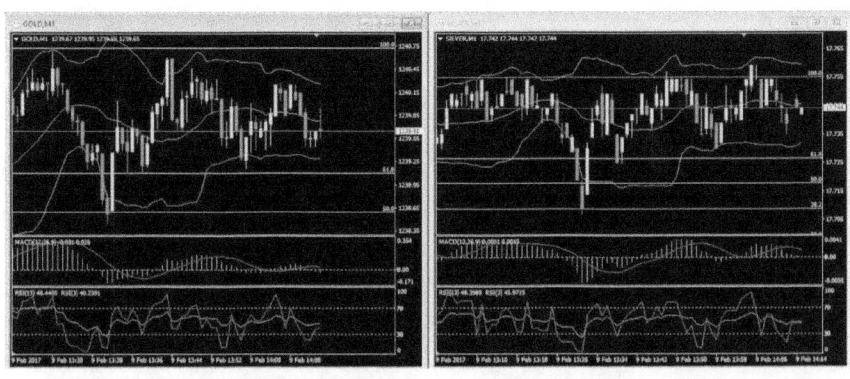

The trading history from these options can be seen below.

| ^ Date | ≑ Asset | ≑ Value | ≑ Operation type | ≑ Expiration time | ≑ Expiry Value | ≑ Amount | ≑ Profit | ≑ Net profit |
|---|---|---|---|---|---|---|---|---|
| 09.02.2017, 14:58:47 | Gold | 1239.75 | ℜ call | 09.02.2017, 15:15:00 | 1239.96 | $ 10.00 | $ 17.50 | $ 7.50 |
| 09.02.2017, 14:58:40 | Silver | 17.7575 | ℜ call | 09.02.2017, 15:15:00 | 17.768 | $ 10.00 | $ 17.30 | $ 7.30 |
| 09.02.2017, 14:58:37 | Silver | 17.7575 | ℜ call | 09.02.2017, 15:15:00 | 17.768 | $ 10.00 | $ 17.30 | $ 7.30 |
| 09.02.2017, 14:56:14 | Silver | 17.7835 | ℜ call | 09.02.2017, 15:15:00 | 17.768 | $ 10.00 | $ 17.30 | $ 7.30 |
| 09.02.2017, 14:56:06 | Gold | 1239.8575 | ℜ call | 09.02.2017, 15:15:00 | 1239.96 | $ 10.00 | $ 17.50 | $ 7.50 |

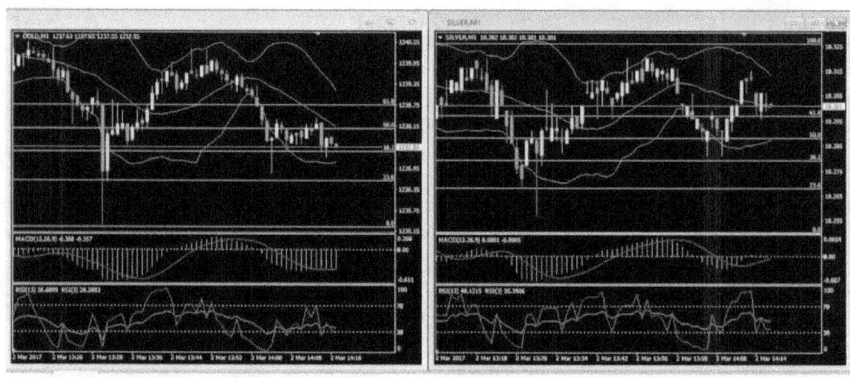

In the charts above you can see a put option on silver and gold. Both assets went out the same direction. There is a trading correlation between them.

# PART IV
# INDICES

It's useful to use US trade indices like Dow Jones, S&P 500, and Nasdaq. European to use include Germany's DAX 30, London's FTSE100, and France's CAC40. The Japanese Nikkei 225 should also be considered.

**S&P 500**

The volatility of the S&P 500 index over the past 30 days is on the historical bottom. This can be alarming. However, if we believe the statistics, the dormant winter period and low volatility in the equity market are behind us. October is, on average, awful for a capital market. According to available data, the average yield of the S&P 500 index in September was negative 0.50%. Let us remember that in 2008, during the height of the financial crisis, the capitulation of the large investment bank Lehman Brothers was in September. We had a low volatility index in the previous month, the high valuation of companies and the decision by the Fed to raise interest rates. It could affect the higher volatility compared to the previous two months.

In the image below, you can see a rising trend line on the S&P 500 during February of 2017. The entry points were

2276.40 and 2276.67, while exit points were 2278.88. This was a 15-minute time frame expiry. It was clear that the price was broken from the 100 Fibonacci level as confirmation of bullish trend line. You can also see that a strong support level has formed at the 61.8 Fibonacci level at 2271. The price also had broken upper Bollinger Bands. The RSI was at 99 level while the moving average convergence divergence (MACD) went out from the oversold zone.

Trading details are shown in the image below, with an investment amount of $10 per trade and a payout of 80%. The retained profit was $8 per trade. Two trades were made in the same direction as a signal that charts analysis was excellent.

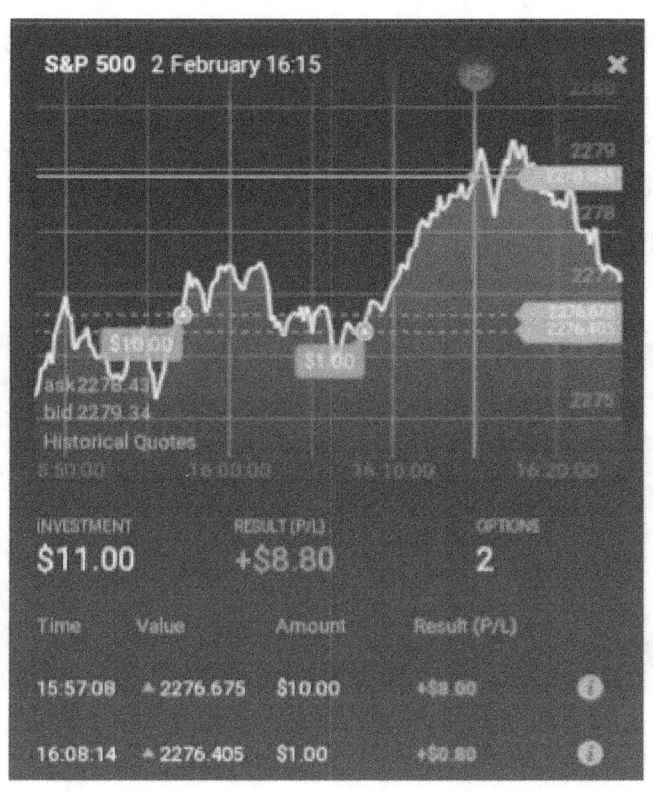

## German DAX30

You can see in the image below a trading DAX30 call option H 2-timeframe expiry. It was supported by a rising trend line with entry points at 11593, while expiry price was 11651 index points. Investment amount was $10 while payout was 65%. Retained profit was made at $6.5 per trade. The indicating signal was when MACD went out from overbought zone while the RSI was 30 level.

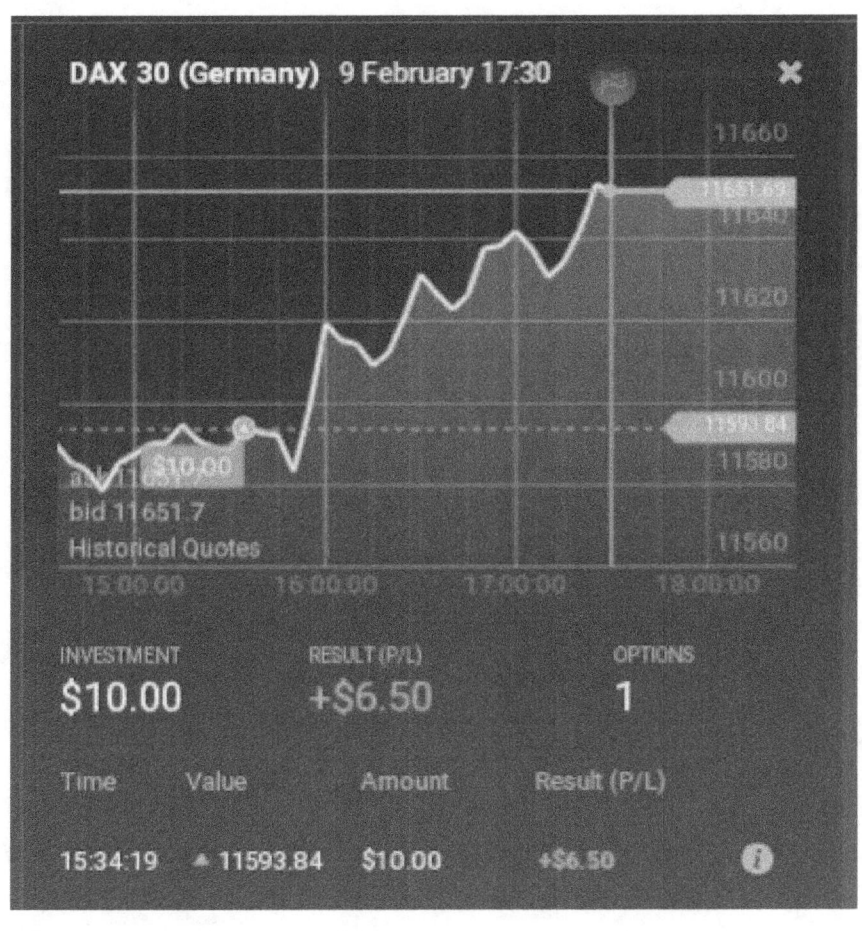

The following trade below had the same situation on the German index DAX30. Three consecutive call option trades we made. They were winning trades. The total investment was at $30, while retained profit was $19.50.

Operations:

| Date | Asset | Value | Operation type | Expiration time | Expiry Value | Amount | Profit | Net profit |
|---|---|---|---|---|---|---|---|---|
| 16.02.2017, 16:02:28 | DAX 30 (Germany) | 11739.05 | call | 16.02.2017, 16:15:00 | 11744.28 | $ 10.00 | $ 16.50 | $ 6.50 |
| 16.02.2017, 16:01:46 | DAX 30 (Germany) | 11740.5 | call | 16.02.2017, 16:15:00 | 11744.28 | $ 10.00 | $ 16.50 | $ 6.50 |
| 16.02.2017, 16:01:00 | DAX 30 (Germany) | 11742.19 | call | 16.02.2017, 16:15:00 | 11744.28 | $ 10.00 | $ 16.50 | $ 6.50 |

## US index Dow Jones

| Date | Asset | Value | Operation type | Expiration time | Expiry Value | Amount | Profit | Net profit |
|---|---|---|---|---|---|---|---|---|
| 26.01.2017, 15:56:30 | DOW JONES 30 | 20093.855 | call | 26.01.2017, 22:00:00 | 20099.71 | $ 10.00 | $ 18.00 | $ 8.00 |
| 26.01.2017, 15:56:20 | DOW JONES 30 | 20092.55 | call | 26.01.2017, 22:00:00 | 20099.71 | $ 1.00 | $ 1.80 | $ 0.80 |

In the above image you can see the call option on Dow Jones 20 minutes time frame expiry. Entry points were 20093 while expiry points were 20099. Investment amount was $11 while retained profit was $8.80. The payout was 80%.

# PART V
# CONCLUSION

There isn't a perfect trading strategy. In the image below you can see a 90% success rate, with 9 winning trades and 1 lost trade.

| * Date | ≑ Asset | ≑ Value | ≑ Operation type | ≑ Expiration time | ≑ Expiry Value | ≑ Amount | ≑ Profit | ≑ Net profit |
|---|---|---|---|---|---|---|---|---|
| 14.02.2017, 14:56:09 | USD/JPY | 113.358 | call | 14.02.2017, 15:15:00 | 113.382 | $ 10.00 | $ 17.00 | $ 7.00 |
| 14.02.2017, 14:56:00 | AUD/USD | 0.768615 | put | 14.02.2017, 15:15:00 | 0.768415 | $ 10.00 | $ 17.90 | $ 7.90 |
| 13.02.2017, 15:00:39 | USD/CHF | 1.0045 | call | 13.02.2017, 15:15:00 | 1.004795 | $ 10.00 | $ 17.50 | $ 7.50 |
| 13.02.2017, 14:59:17 | USD/CHF | 1.004605 | call | 13.02.2017, 15:15:00 | 1.004795 | $ 10.00 | $ 17.50 | $ 7.50 |
| 13.02.2017, 14:59:13 | GBP/USD | 1.25143 | put | 13.02.2017, 15:15:00 | 1.249815 | $ 10.00 | $ 17.50 | $ 7.50 |
| 13.02.2017, 14:57:03 | GBP/USD | 1.25135 | put | 13.02.2017, 15:15:00 | 1.249815 | $ 10.00 | $ 17.50 | $ 7.50 |
| 13.02.2017, 14:54:55 | GBP/USD | 1.25121 | put | 13.02.2017, 15:15:00 | 1.249815 | $ 10.00 | $ 17.50 | $ 7.50 |
| 13.02.2017, 14:54:44 | USD/CHF | 1.004705 | call | 13.02.2017, 15:15:00 | 1.004795 | $ 10.00 | $ 17.50 | $ 7.50 |
| 10.02.2017, 14:59:06 | USD/CAD | 1.309235 | call | 10.02.2017, 15:15:00 | 1.3068 | $ 10.00 | $ 0.00 | $ -10.00 |
| 10.02.2017, 14:56:53 | EUR/GBP | 0.851995 | call | 10.02.2017, 15:15:00 | 0.852025 | $ 10.00 | $ 17.50 | $ 7.50 |

The next image shows a 100% success rate, 10 consecutive winning trades.

| * Date | ≑ Asset | ≑ Value | ≑ Operation type | ≑ Expiration time | ≑ Expiry Value | ≑ Amount | ≑ Profit | ≑ Net profit |
|---|---|---|---|---|---|---|---|---|
| 09.02.2017, 15:34:19 | DAX 30 (Germany) | 11593.84 | call | 09.02.2017, 17:30:00 | 11651.69 | $ 10.00 | $ 16.90 | $ 6.90 |
| 09.02.2017, 14:58:47 | Gold | 1239.75 | call | 09.02.2017, 15:15:00 | 1239.96 | $ 10.00 | $ 17.50 | $ 7.50 |
| 09.02.2017, 14:58:40 | Silver | 17.7575 | call | 09.02.2017, 15:15:00 | 17.768 | $ 10.00 | $ 17.30 | $ 7.30 |
| 09.02.2017, 14:58:37 | Silver | 17.7575 | call | 09.02.2017, 15:15:00 | 17.768 | $ 10.00 | $ 17.30 | $ 7.30 |
| 09.02.2017, 14:56:14 | Silver | 17.7635 | call | 09.02.2017, 15:15:00 | 17.768 | $ 10.00 | $ 17.30 | $ 7.30 |
| 09.02.2017, 14:56:05 | Gold | 1239.8575 | call | 09.02.2017, 15:15:00 | 1239.96 | $ 10.00 | $ 17.50 | $ 7.50 |
| 08.02.2017, 15:01:19 | GBP/JPY | 140.1135 | call | 08.02.2017, 15:15:00 | 140.269 | $ 10.00 | $ 17.50 | $ 7.50 |
| 08.02.2017, 14:55:38 | EUR/USD | 1.06661 | call | 08.02.2017, 15:15:00 | 1.06817 | $ 10.00 | $ 17.70 | $ 7.70 |
| 08.02.2017, 14:53:28 | EUR/USD | 1.066765 | call | 08.02.2017, 15:15:00 | 1.06817 | $ 10.00 | $ 17.70 | $ 7.70 |
| 08.02.2017, 14:53:03 | GBP/JPY | 140.1015 | call | 08.02.2017, 15:15:00 | 140.269 | $ 10.00 | $ 17.50 | $ 7.50 |

The next image shows an 80% success rate, 8 winning and 2 lost trades.

| Date | Asset | Value | Operation type | Expiration time | Expiry Value | Amount | Profit | Net profit |
|---|---|---|---|---|---|---|---|---|
| 07.02.2017, 15:00:47 | USD/JPY | 112.3685 | call | 07.02.2017, 15:15:00 | 112.3825 | $ 10.00 | $ 17.00 | $ 7.00 |
| 07.02.2017, 15:00:29 | AUD/USD | 0.762025 | put | 07.02.2017, 15:15:00 | 0.76164 | $ 10.00 | $ 17.90 | $ 7.90 |
| 07.02.2017, 14:59:08 | USD/JPY | 112.395 | call | 07.02.2017, 15:15:00 | 112.3825 | $ 10.00 | $ 0.00 | $ -10.00 |
| 06.02.2017, 14:53:34 | GBP/USD | 1.245875 | put | 06.02.2017, 15:15:00 | 1.245395 | $ 10.00 | $ 17.50 | $ 7.50 |
| 06.02.2017, 14:53:30 | USD/CHF | 0.995015 | call | 06.02.2017, 15:15:00 | 0.995625 | $ 10.00 | $ 17.50 | $ 7.50 |
| 03.02.2017, 15:07:08 | EUR/GBP | 0.86204 | put | 03.02.2017, 15:15:00 | 0.861795 | $ 10.00 | $ 17.50 | $ 7.50 |
| 03.02.2017, 15:06:44 | EUR/GBP | 0.86181 | put | 03.02.2017, 15:15:00 | 0.861795 | $ 10.00 | $ 17.50 | $ 7.50 |
| 03.02.2017, 15:06:40 | USD/CAD | 1.301535 | call | 03.02.2017, 15:15:00 | 1.30241 | $ 10.00 | $ 17.30 | $ 7.30 |
| 03.02.2017, 15:03:23 | USD/CAD | 1.3017 | call | 03.02.2017, 15:15:00 | 1.30241 | $ 10.00 | $ 17.30 | $ 7.30 |
| 03.02.2017, 15:03:04 | EUR/GBP | 0.86175 | put | 03.02.2017, 15:15:00 | 0.861795 | $ 10.00 | $ 0.00 | $ -10.00 |

The next image is also shows an 80% success rate, 8 winning trades and 2 lost trades.

| Date | Asset | Value | Operation type | Expiration time | Expiry Value | Amount | Profit | Net profit |
|---|---|---|---|---|---|---|---|---|
| 01.02.2017, 14:55:25 | GBP/JPY | 143.7275 | put | 01.02.2017, 15:15:00 | 143.641 | $ 10.00 | $ 17.50 | $ 7.50 |
| 31.01.2017, 15:08:07 | AUD/USD | 0.75751 | put | 31.01.2017, 15:15:00 | 0.75689 | $ 10.00 | $ 17.90 | $ 7.90 |
| 31.01.2017, 15:08:04 | AUD/USD | 0.75752 | put | 31.01.2017, 15:15:00 | 0.75689 | $ 10.00 | $ 17.90 | $ 7.90 |
| 31.01.2017, 15:07:38 | USD/JPY | 113.2885 | call | 31.01.2017, 15:15:00 | 113.321 | $ 10.00 | $ 17.00 | $ 7.00 |
| 31.01.2017, 15:07:27 | AUD/USD | 0.75748 | put | 31.01.2017, 15:15:00 | 0.75689 | $ 10.00 | $ 17.90 | $ 7.90 |
| 31.01.2017, 15:01:40 | USD/JPY | 113.297 | call | 31.01.2017, 15:15:00 | 113.321 | $ 10.00 | $ 17.00 | $ 7.00 |
| 31.01.2017, 15:01:08 | AUD/USD | 0.757285 | put | 31.01.2017, 15:15:00 | 0.75689 | $ 10.00 | $ 17.90 | $ 7.90 |
| 30.01.2017, 15:03:36 | GBP/USD | 1.253385 | put | 30.01.2017, 15:15:00 | 1.253055 | $ 10.00 | $ 17.50 | $ 7.50 |
| 30.01.2017, 15:03:33 | USD/CHF | 1.00097 | call | 30.01.2017, 15:15:00 | 1.000945 | $ 10.00 | $ 0.00 | $ -10.00 |
| 30.01.2017, 15:02:41 | GBP/USD | 1.253005 | put | 30.01.2017, 15:15:00 | 1.253055 | $ 10.00 | $ 17.50 | $ 7.50 |
| 30.01.2017, 15:02:29 | GBP/USD | 1.25299 | put | 30.01.2017, 15:15:00 | 1.253055 | $ 10.00 | $ 0.00 | $ -10.00 |

The next image shows 100% success rate, 10 consecutive winning trades.

The last image shows the perfect trading strategy, 100% success rate and 7 consecutive winning trades in one day only.

AUD/USD 7 March 15:47
0.75961
0.75959
$500.00
0.7595
0.7594
bid 0.75962
Historical Quotes
15:46:00
15:46:30
15:47:00
INVESTMENT
$1,000.00
RESULT (P/L)
+$900.00
OPTIONS
2
Time
Value
Amount
Result (P/L)
15:46:02 0.759585 $500.00 +$450.00
15:46:08 0.759590 $500.00 +$450.00

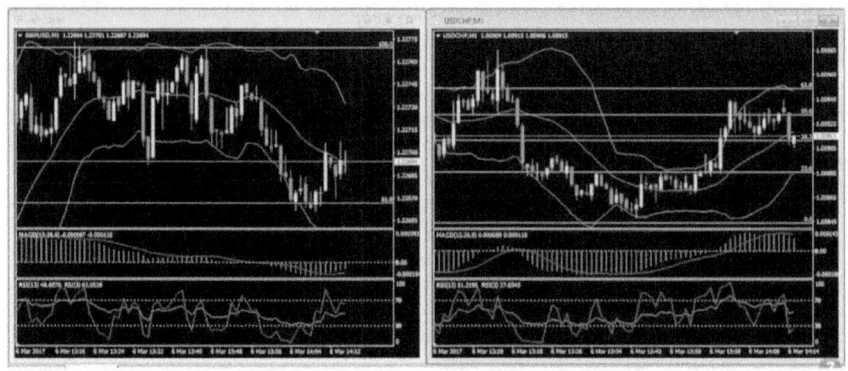

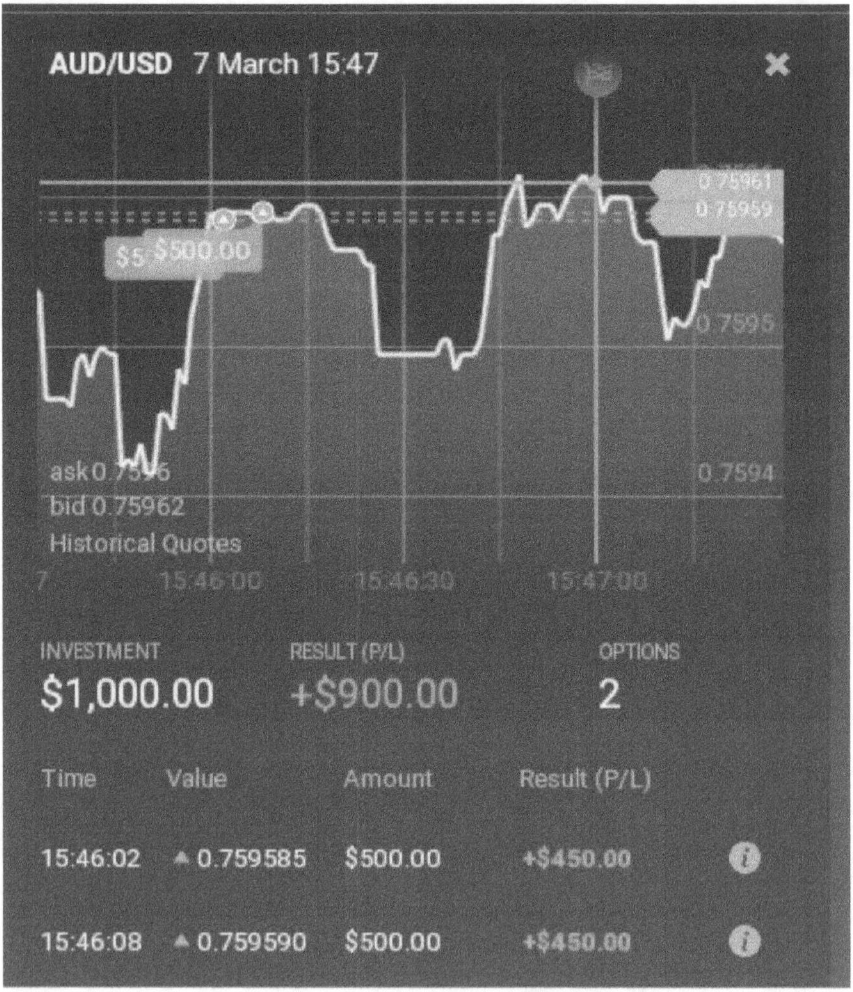

Operations:

| Date | Asset | Value | Operation type | Expiration time | Expiry Value | Amount | Profit | Net profit |
|---|---|---|---|---|---|---|---|---|
| 08.03.2017, 15:50:42 | EUR/USD | 1.055585 | call | 08.03.2017, 15:52:00 | 1.055915 | $ 1 000.00 | $ 1 850.00 | $ 850.00 |
| 08.03.2017, 15:47:21 | GBP/JPY | 139.471 | put | 08.03.2017, 15:48:00 | 139.4555 | $ 1 000.00 | $ 1 850.00 | $ 850.00 |
| 08.03.2017, 15:45:48 | GBP/JPY | 139.4405 | call | 08.03.2017, 15:47:00 | 139.485 | $ 1 000.00 | $ 1 850.00 | $ 850.00 |
| 08.03.2017, 15:44:13 | GBP/JPY | 139.3815 | call | 08.03.2017, 15:45:00 | 139.3865 | $ 500.00 | $ 925.00 | $ 425.00 |

With trading you will have good days, and you will have not so good days. The important thing is that you continue to learn, that you build up the experience you need to spot the patterns in the market. Listen to what the numbers and candlesticks are telling you. All the information you need is in there.

You now have all the information you need to get started! Make sure you always have an attitude for hard work and learning. If you fail enough times you will eventually become successful. Be sure to minimize risk and practice on a demo account before setting out to make real money. Good luck!

www.ingramcontent.com/pod-product-compliance
Lightning Source LLC
Chambersburg PA
CBHW070209230526
45471CB00002B/888